...ars, people from around the world have come to explore the Arctic and Antarctic. Here are some of their stories.

Richard E. Byrd
Byrd becomes the first to fly to the South Pole and back from his base on the Ross Ice Shelf. The journey takes 18 hours and 41 minutes.

Caroline Mikkelsen
Caroline Mikkelsen becomes the first woman to set foot on Antarctica where her expedition raises the flag for Norway.

Fiennes and his team

Sir Ranulph Fiennes
Fiennes and his Transglobe Expedition become the first to travel around the world between the North and South Poles.

| 1914–17 | 1929 | 1935 | 1937 | 1957–58 | 1979–82 |

Nukapinguaq
Nukapinguaq is one of the greatest high-Arctic guides. He is part of many major expeditions between 1913 and 1938, including the British Arctic Expedition of 1937.

Vivian Fuchs and Edmund Hillary
As part of the Commonwealth Trans-Antarctic Expedition, Fuchs and Hillary lead a team that makes the first overland crossing of Antarctica.

Endurance

Sir Ernest Shackleton
Shackleton's ship, Endurance, is crushed by pack ice. Against the odds, Shackleton leads his whole crew to safety.

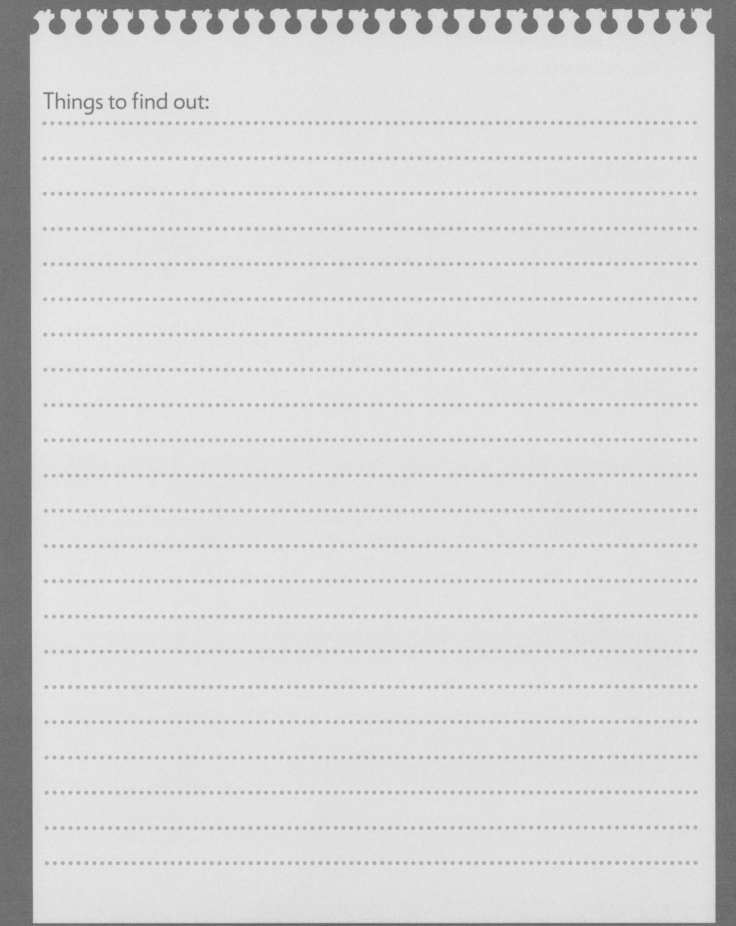

Things to find out:

DK findout!

Arctic and Antarctic

Author: Anita Ganeri
Consultant: Simon Morley

Senior editors Carrie Love, Roohi Sehgal
US editors Shannon Beatty, Mindy Fichter
Project editors Robin Moul, Radhika Haswani
Editorial support Madhurima Chatterjee
Project art editors Eleanor Bates, Roohi Rais
Art editors Bhagyashree Nayak, Mohd Zishan
Publishing coordinator Issy Walsh
Jacket designer Rashika Kachroo
DTP designers Sachin Gupta,
Syed Md Farhan, Vikram Singh
Project picture researcher Sakshi Saluja
Production editor Abi Maxwell
Production controller Isabell Schart
Managing editors Penny Smith, Monica Saigal
Managing art editor Ivy Sengupta
Delhi team heads Glenda Fernandes, Malavika Talukder
Deputy art director Mabel Chan
Publishing director Sarah Larter

Educational consultant Jacqueline Harris

First American Edition, 2022
Published in the United States by DK Publishing
1450 Broadway, Suite 801, New York, NY 10018

Copyright © 2022 Dorling Kindersley Limited
DK, a Division of Penguin Random House LLC
22 23 24 25 26 10 9 8 7 6 5 4 3 2 1
001–327009–June/2022

A catalog record for this book is available
from the Library of Congress.
ISBN: 978-0-7440-5653-2 (Hardcover)
ISBN: 978-0-7440-5652-5 (Paperback)

DK books are available at special discounts when purchased in bulk
for sales promotions, premiums, fundraising, or educational use.
For details, contact: DK Publishing Special Markets,
1450 Broadway, Suite 801, New York, NY 10018
SpecialSales@dk.com
Printed and bound in China

For the curious
www.dk.com

This book was made with Forest
Stewardship Council™ certified
paper—one small step in DK's
commitment to a sustainable future.
For more information go to
www.dk.com/our-green-pledge

The scale boxes on pages 16–17,
18–19, and 20–21 of this book show
you how big an animal is compared
to a person who is 6 ft (1.8 m) tall.

》Scale

Contents

4 Polar regions

6 Land and sea ice

8 Glaciers and icebergs

10 Auroras

12 Polar bears

14 Penguins

16 Land mammals

18 Sea giants

20 Polar birds

22 Unusual animals

24 Flora and fauna

26 Food web

Antarctic krill

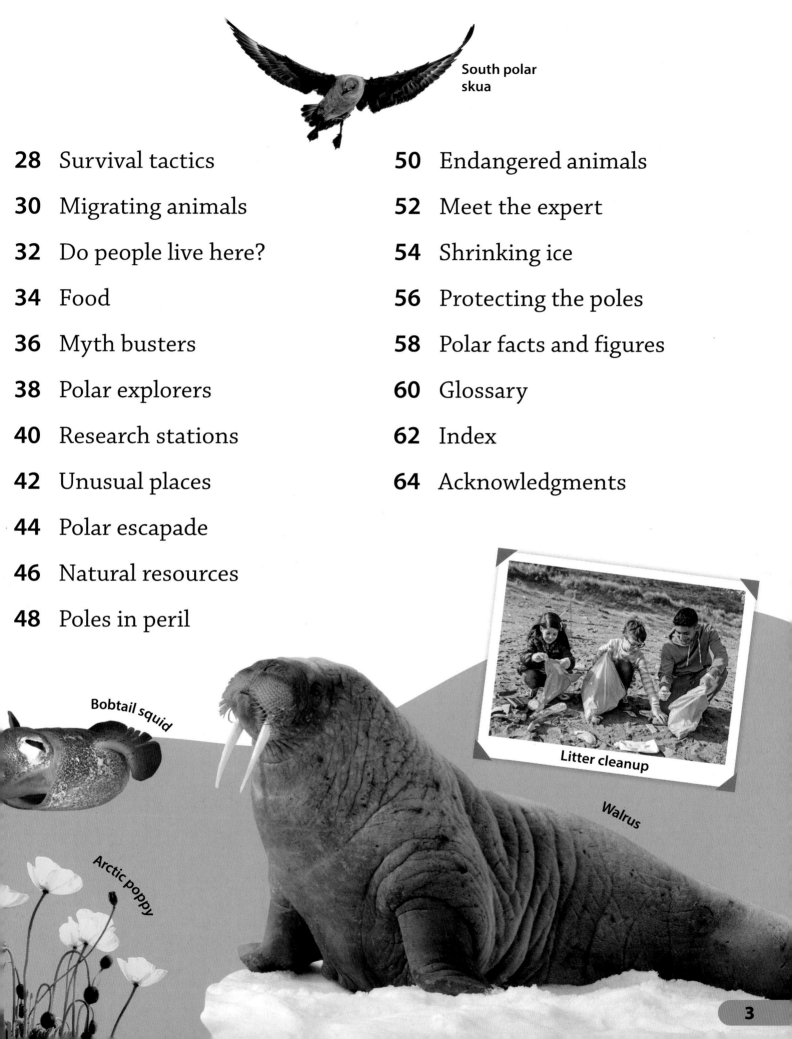

South polar skua

28 Survival tactics

30 Migrating animals

32 Do people live here?

34 Food

36 Myth busters

38 Polar explorers

40 Research stations

42 Unusual places

44 Polar escapade

46 Natural resources

48 Poles in peril

50 Endangered animals

52 Meet the expert

54 Shrinking ice

56 Protecting the poles

58 Polar facts and figures

60 Glossary

62 Index

64 Acknowledgments

Bobtail squid

Arctic poppy

Walrus

Litter cleanup

Polar regions

Located at the very ends of the Earth, the polar regions—the Arctic and Antarctic—are among the coldest and windiest places on the planet. They are so cold partly because the sun's rays hit them at an angle and spread out over a wide area. Additionally, the white color of ice reflects the sun's heat back into space.

! **WOW!**

In the Antarctic, average winter temperatures fall below −77°F (−60°C)!

The Arctic Ocean is partly frozen for most of the year.

I can **blend** in with the **snow** anytime!

Where on Earth?
The Arctic is the region around the North Pole, at the Earth's northernmost point. The Antarctic is the region around the South Pole, at the southernmost point.

The Arctic
The Arctic includes the Arctic Ocean, the northern parts of North America, Europe, and Asia, as well as the island of Greenland. A huge ice sheet covers much of Greenland.

Vegetation

Despite the ice and cold, many types of plants grow at the poles. In the Arctic, there are grasses, mosses, and flowering plants. In the Antarctic, there are mainly lichens, mosses, and liverworts.

Flowering plants of the Arctic

Lichen in the Antarctic

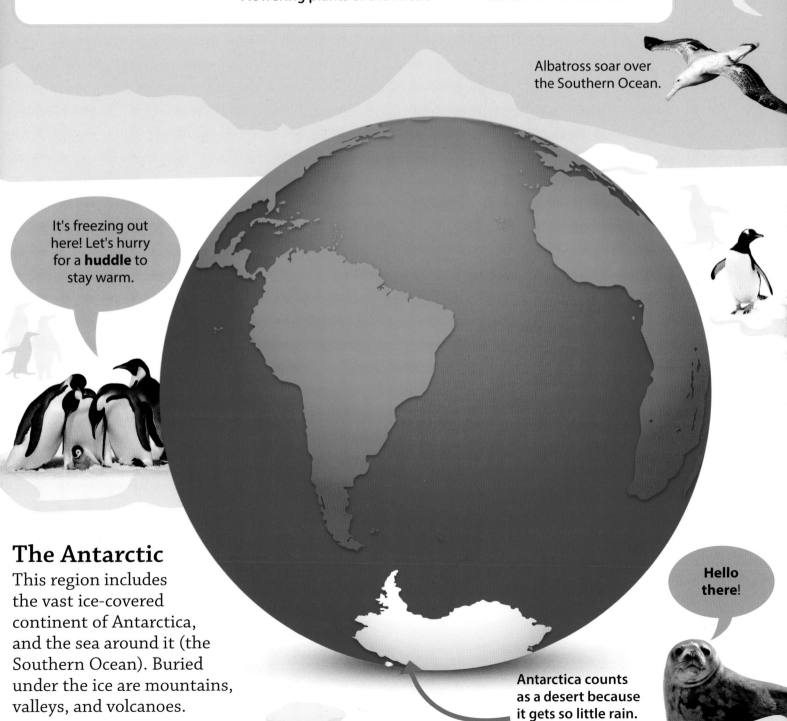

Albatross soar over the Southern Ocean.

It's freezing out here! Let's hurry for a **huddle** to stay warm.

The Antarctic

This region includes the vast ice-covered continent of Antarctica, and the sea around it (the Southern Ocean). Buried under the ice are mountains, valleys, and volcanoes.

Hello there!

Antarctica counts as a desert because it gets so little rain.

Land and sea ice

Large areas of the Arctic and Antarctic are covered with different types of ice, both on land and out at sea. Some of this polar ice melts in summer, while some stays frozen all year round.

More than 70 percent of Greenland is covered in an ice sheet.

Ice sheets

Ice sheets are vast areas of ice on land. They are so big that there are only two in the world: one covering Antarctica, and one covering most of Greenland.

Greenland ice sheet

The Ross Ice Shelf is around the same size as France.

Ross Ice Shelf, Antarctica

Ice shelves

An ice shelf is a huge slab of ice that stays fixed to an ice sheet or glacier, but floats on the sea.

Ice caps

An ice cap is a thick layer of ice that covers a large area of land. It can even bury large natural features, such as mountains.

Land ice

The tops of mountains can be seen sticking above the ice.

Ice caps in Antarctica

Arctic brash ice

Brash ice

Brash ice is a jumble of broken pieces of sea ice. It often forms when ice floes smash into each other.

What is permafrost?

In the land around the Arctic Ocean, the ground beneath the surface is frozen all year long. Even in summer, only the top few inches thaw.

Frozen ground in Norway

Pack ice forms when salt water freezes. It drifts on the surface in pieces.

Sea ice

Ice floes

An ice floe is a large, flat piece of sea ice. Giant floes can measure 6.5 miles (10 km) across. The smallest floes are called ice cakes.

Sea birds on an ice floe

Ice floes can make the water very dangerous for ships.

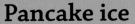
Pancake ice

Pancake ice

Some pieces of sea ice are flat and round, like pancakes. They have raised edges because their rims turn up when they bash into each other at sea.

Flowing glaciers

From the ice sheet, a glacier flows very slowly toward the sea. It is pulled along by its own weight and the force of gravity.

Breaking away

At the coast, an iceberg breaks off the end of the glacier with a loud "boom" and "crack." This is called "calving."

Glaciers and icebergs

Glaciers are enormous rivers of ice that grow over hundreds, or even thousands, of years. At the poles, they flow out from ice sheets toward the coast. There, massive chunks of ice break off and float away to sea. These are called icebergs.

! WOW!

An iceberg bigger than the island of Majorca calved in Antarctica in 2021.

Floating away

As the iceberg floats away to sea, only around a tenth of it shows above the surface. The rest is hidden underwater.

Iceberg shapes

Icebergs come in different shapes. Some are block- or wedge-shaped, while others are dome-shaped, with rounded tops. Many have flat tops while some others are jagged or pointed.

Iceberg in Antarctica

Drifting

An iceberg is carried along by wind and ocean currents. It can drift for thousands of miles (kilometers) before it finally melts.

Melting away

As the iceberg moves into warmer water, it starts to break up into smaller chunks and melts.

Auroras

Look up at the night sky near the poles and you might see spectacular light shows. They occur when particles, too small to see, stream away from the sun and disturb Earth's magnetic field (a force field around the planet). When they collide with gas particles in our atmosphere, their energy turns into natural glowing lights called "auroras."

Aurora patterns

Auroras illuminate the night sky with huge displays of natural light. But not every light show is the same. Just like clouds, auroras take different forms and shapes, from large patches of glowing color to long arcs of light stretching across the horizon.

The Aurora Borealis form "bands"

Smooth bands
Many formations begin as a simple curved light called an "arc." Bands are a type of arc and they can be smooth, curved, or twist at the ends.

Colorful night lights
Auroras are mostly green, but they can also be yellow, blue, red, and pink.

Aurora Borealis dancing across the sky, creating "curtains"

A vibrant "crown" illuminating the sky

Curtain
Rays can appear as thick blankets of light, or as vertical columns beaming down on land. These can be described as "curtains."

Crown
When multiple rays appear to spread out from a central point, they form a "starburst" or "crown" pattern overhead.

Polar bears

Polar bears are the world's largest bears. Powerful hunters, they search for seals on the ice and in the water. They are superbly adapted for Arctic life, and can swim long distances, using their huge front paws as paddles.

A dense fur coat and a thick layer of blubber (fat) under the skin help to keep the bear warm and waterproof.

Why don't polar bears freeze?

The hairs in a polar bear's coat are hollow and filled with air. They trap the sun's heat and help the bear to stay buoyant (afloat) in the water.

A hollow hair under a microscope

Habitat
Polar bears live in and around the Arctic Ocean. In winter, females dig dens in the ice where they give birth to their cubs (young).

A polar bear has a small head and ears to help cut down the amount of heat it loses from its body.

A cub leaving the den

Diet
Polar bears spend more than half of their life hunting. They prey mainly on bearded and ringed seals that are rich in nourishing fat.

Play-fighting helps cubs get ready for adult life.

Male cubs play-fighting

Behavior
These polar bears are play-fighting, but rival males can sometimes fight to the death over prey or to defend their territory.

Penguins

They're the most famous birds in Antarctica, perfectly adapted for life in the cold. Coats of oily, overlapping feathers and thick blubber under their skin help to keep them warm.

A colony of chinstrap penguins

Colonies

Most penguins live and breed in large groups, called colonies. A penguin colony can be made up of hundreds of thousands of birds.

Penguins sometimes eat ice

Diet

Penguins feed on fish, krill, crabs, and squid that they catch in the ocean. In turn, they are hunted by predators, such as orcas and leopard seals.

Chicks lose their fluffy feathers so they can grow a waterproof coat.

A couple of adult emperor penguins and chicks huddle together for warmth on the ice.

A gentoo penguin chick moulting

Molting

Molting is when a bird naturally loses its feathers and grows new ones. A penguin chick molts when it loses its baby feathers. Adult penguins also molt once a year to maintain sturdy, waterproof coats.

Penguins in shallow water

Swimming

Penguins cannot fly and look clumsy on land. In the water, though, they are speedy swimmers, using their wings as flippers.

REALLY?

! A mature **emperor penguin** can stand more than **3 ft (1 m)** tall.

Land mammals

In addition to polar bears, many other mammals also live on the land around the frozen Arctic Ocean. These mammals have a range of features to help them survive in their harsh, icy home.

FACT FILE

» **Location:** Arctic

» **Diet:** Grasses, sedges

» **Fun fact:** If there is danger, adult musk oxen form a circle around their young.

Musk ox

Musk oxen live in large herds. Their long, shaggy, thick fur coats, made of two layers, protect them from the cold.

Ermine

Also known as a stoat, the ermine has a reddish-brown coat that turns white in the winter. This helps it to camouflage among the ice and snow.

FACT FILE

» **Location:** Arctic

» **Diet:** Small mammals, small birds

» **Fun fact:** The tip of an ermine's tail is always black, even in the winter.

An ermine with its white winter coat

» Scale

Wolverine

This fierce mammal lives in a den dug into a snowdrift or among rocks. It travels long distances every day to hunt for food.

» Scale

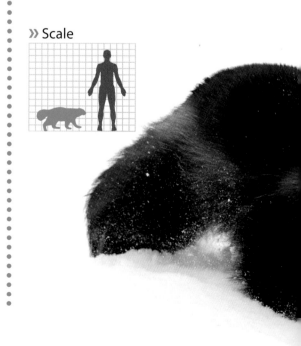

The outer layer of fur reaches almost to the ground.

» Scale
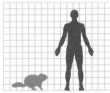

Arctic ground squirrel

Arctic ground squirrels hibernate during winter. Safe in their burrows, they live off fat stored in their bodies.

An Arctic ground squirrel on the lookout for danger.

» Scale

FACT FILE

» **Location:** Arctic
....
» **Diet:** Seeds, fruit
....
» **Fun fact:** Arctic ground squirrels live in large, sociable colonies.

FACT FILE

» **Location:** Arctic
....
» **Diet:** Caribou, hares, birds, eggs, fruit
....
» **Fun fact:** A wolverine's super-strong jaws can crunch through frozen meat.

Wolverines are related to stoats and weasels.

Arctic fox

This fox's thick fur is brown in summer, and turns white in winter. It has furry pads on its feet for walking over the ice and snow.

FACT FILE

» **Location:** Arctic
....
» **Diet:** Small rodents, baby seals, carrion
....
» **Fun fact:** Arctic foxes like to eat leftovers from polar bears' meals.

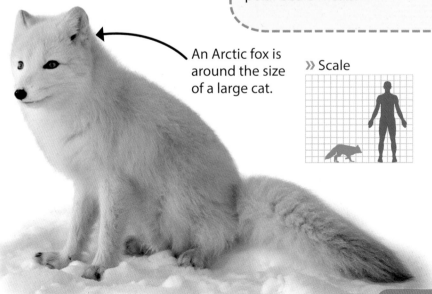

An Arctic fox is around the size of a large cat.

» Scale

Sea giants

Marine mammals are found in both the Arctic and Antarctic. Some are adapted to living completely in water. Others swim and dive for food in the sea, but also spend time on the land or the ice to rest and breed.

Some sea giants **migrate**, but others live in polar regions **all year long.**

Walrus

A walrus's bristly whiskers are very sensitive, and help the walrus to find food in the dark Arctic waters.

» Scale

FACT FILE

» **Location:** Arctic

» **Diet:** Shellfish, worms, sea snails

» **Fun fact:** Walruses huddle together in huge herds on ice floes.

A male walrus weighs around three times more than a cow.

A female walrus can also grow tusks.

Narwhal

A narwhal is a type of porpoise with a long, spiral tusk. The tusk is a tooth that grows though the narwhal's upper lip.

A tusk can grow to 9 ft (3 m) long.

» Scale

Beluga whale

Newborn belugas are dark gray, but turn into all-white adults. This helps them to blend in with the ice floes and icebergs.

Belugas are very vocal.

» Scale

Southern elephant seal

These seals get their name from their trunklike noses. They weigh around as much as an Asian elephant.

They are also the largest seals.

» Scale

Leopard seal

Leopard seals are fierce predators, with strong jaws and sharp teeth for catching their prey.

» Scale

Leopard seals are amazing swimmers.

Polar birds

Penguins may be the most famous of all polar birds, but the Arctic and Antarctic are home to many other bird species. Some are year-round residents, while others only visit in the summer.

WOW!

There are **22 species** of **albatross**. Most of them are **endangered**.

South polar skua

These skuas migrate to the Antarctic coast to breed. They catch fish by diving or by plucking fish from the ocean's surface.

» Scale

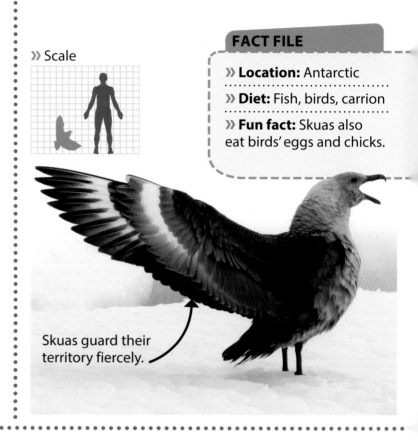

FACT FILE

» **Location:** Antarctic

» **Diet:** Fish, birds, carrion

» **Fun fact:** Skuas also eat birds' eggs and chicks.

Skuas guard their territory fiercely.

An albatross glides on its long, slender wings.

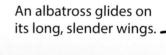

An albatross uses its sense of smell to find food.

Albatross

Using updrafts of wind, an albatross can soar for hours on end, without having to beat its wings.

Atlantic puffin

Atlantic puffins are very sociable birds. They nest in colonies on rocky coasts and islands, and feed in large groups, known as "rafts" out at sea.

FACT FILE

» **Location:** Arctic

» **Diet:** Fish

» **Fun fact:** A puffin's bill is lined with spikes for gripping fish.

Puffins lay their eggs in burrows in the ground.

» Scale

» Scale

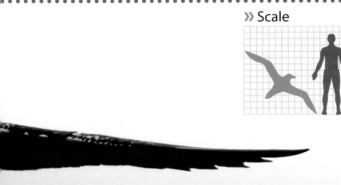

FACT FILE

» **Location:** Antarctic

» **Diet:** Fish, squid, plankton

» **Fun fact:** The wandering albatross has the widest wingspan of any bird.

Snowy owl

Snowy owls have long, thick feathers that cover their whole bodies, including their toes and most of their bills.

Owls have sharp hearing and eyesight.

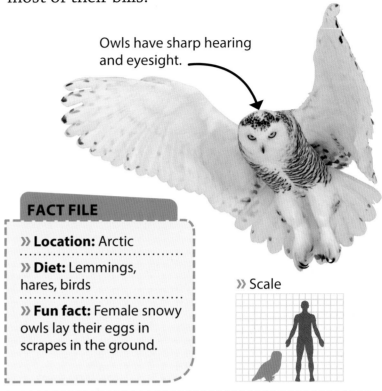

FACT FILE

» **Location:** Arctic

» **Diet:** Lemmings, hares, birds

» **Fun fact:** Female snowy owls lay their eggs in scrapes in the ground.

» Scale

King eider

King eiders are large sea ducks, sometimes seen resting on ice floes. They are well adapted for swimming and diving in the near freezing ocean.

FACT FILE

» **Location:** Arctic

» **Diet:** Mollusks, insect larvae

» **Fun fact:** These birds migrate to the Arctic to breed in the summer.

» Scale

King eiders mostly forage for food at sea.

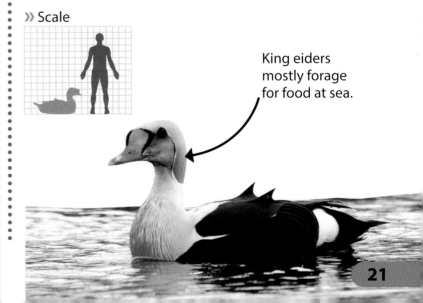

Unusual animals

If you were asked to name a polar animal, you would most likely say a penguin or polar bear. But the Arctic and Antarctic are home to many other creatures. They live on land and in the sea, and have evolved special features to help them survive.

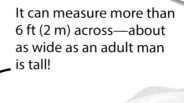
It can measure more than 6 ft (2 m) across—about as wide as an adult man is tall!

The lion's mane jellyfish lives in cold Arctic waters.

Antarctic springtail
Antarctic springtails are among the biggest land animals in Antarctica, even though they are smaller than a pinhead!

Lion's mane jellyfish
This is one of the largest types of jellyfish. It uses its long, trailing tentacles to sting and kill its prey.

Springtails live under rocks. They feed on fungus and bacteria.

Arctic woolly bear caterpillar

This caterpillar spends most of its life frozen. It thaws out to change into an adult moth in the summer months.

Antarctic icefish

An icefish's blood contains chemicals that prevent it from freezing. This means it can survive the icy Antarctic waters.

An icefish

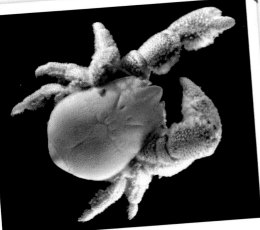

The Hoff crab was discovered in 2010.

Hoff crab

The hairy Hoff crab lives deep in the Southern Ocean, around fountains of hot water, called vents.

Its legs are around 10 in (25 cm) long.

Antarctic sea spider

Antarctic sea spiders live at the bottom of the Southern Ocean. These giants grow as big as dinner plates!

Flora and fauna

Despite the harsh conditions, some plants can still survive at the poles. They have adapted to life with freezing cold, howling winds, and icy soils. These plants provide food for insects, such as butterflies and bees, as well as birds and mammals.

Antarctic midge

The tiny Antarctic midge is one of very few insects that can live in extreme cold. Its larvae burrow into patches of moss, and spend half the year frozen solid.

Purple saxifrage

Clumps of purple saxifrage cover some Arctic rocks. Like many polar plants, purple saxifrage grows low to the ground to avoid being blown away by strong winds.

Arctic fritillary

Female Arctic fritillary butterflies lay their eggs on the underside of plant leaves. When the caterpillars hatch, they munch on the leaves. Adults feed on plant nectar.

Arctic poppy

Summer is short in the Arctic. Arctic poppies bloom quickly, as soon as the warmer weather comes. Their flowers turn toward the sun, soaking up heat and light.

Arctic bumblebee

Bumblebees help to pollinate plants. Arctic bees "shiver" their big flight muscles to warm themselves up enough to fly from flower to flower.

Bzzzz

Antarctic hair grass

Many different flowering plants live in the Arctic. But only two types can survive in Antarctica. One of them, hair grass, mostly grows on rocks around penguin colonies.

ANTARCTIC PEARLWORT

The other flowering plant in Antarctica is pearlwort. It has small, yellow flowers and grows in clumps on rocks. Like hair grass, it is only found along ice-free coasts.

Food web

Plants and animals are linked together by what they eat. The links form a food chain, and when several food chains join up, they make a food web. Here is an example of an Arctic food web.

Phytoplankton

In spring, the ice covering the Arctic Ocean starts to melt. Vast numbers of tiny algae, called phytoplankton, begin to bloom in the sea.

Whales

Despite their huge size, whales mostly feed on small animals, such as krill. They may also eat some fish species.

Humpback whale

Seals

In the Arctic, a seal's diet can include krill, fish, and squid. In turn, seals are the prey of orcas and polar bears.

Harbor seal

Walruses

A walrus's favorite food is shellfish, which it forages from the sea bed. It also eats crabs, fish, worms, and sea cucumbers.

Walrus

Zooplankton

Zooplankton are tiny sea animals, such as krill, that graze on phytoplankton. In turn, krill are eaten by fish, seabirds, and whales.

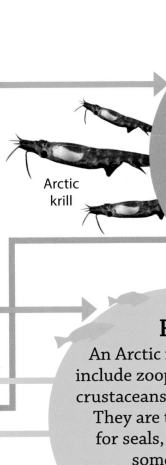

Arctic krill

Arctic tern

Seabirds

Most seabirds feed on fish. Some birds snatch their prey from the surface, while others dive. They may also eat krill, squid, and shellfish.

Fish

An Arctic fish's diet may include zooplankton, squid, crustaceans, and other fish. They are the main food for seals, seabirds, and some whales.

Atlantic cod

Squid

Most squid feed on fish, crustaceans, and mollusks. They may be eaten by fish, seals, and some whale species.

Bobtail squid

Orcas and polar bears

In every polar food chain, orcas and polar bears are the top predators. Polar bears mostly hunt seals. Orcas hunt seals and young whales.

Orca

Polar bear

Survival tactics

In both the Arctic and Antarctic, animals need to be tough to survive. Clever tactics and special features allow them to stay warm, find food and mates, and keep safe from predators.

Thick fur
Polar bears and Arctic foxes are just some of the animals that have thick fur to keep out the cold. A polar bear has a very thick undercoat, and longer, outer hairs.

Staying together
Living in a big group is one way to survive in the cold at the poles. Penguins huddle together for warmth, and to protect themselves and their young from predators.

Cunning camouflage
To blend in with their surroundings, Arctic foxes, hares, and ptarmigan change color. In winter, they turn white, and in summer, they turn brown.

Excellent eyesight

Some animals rely on their sense of smell to find prey and sniff out danger, but others use their eyes. Snowy owls use their excellent eyesight to spot prey on the icy ground below.

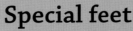

I see you!

Special feet

Hairy or bumpy feet give polar animals a better grip on the slippery ground. A caribou's toes spread out wide like snowshoes so it can walk across ice and snow.

Blubber layer

Many polar animals have a thick layer of yellowish fat, called blubber, under their skins. It helps to keep them warm, especially in the water.

Antifreeze chemical

It is freezing cold in the polar seas, but many fish have special chemicals in their blood. These chemicals stop their blood from freezing.

Migrating animals

Some animals live at the poles all year long. Thousands of other birds and mammals visit in summer, when the weather is warmer. They come to make use of the rich food supply, and to find safe places to nest and have their young.

Arctic terns, Arctic

These terns fly to the Arctic for summer in the Northern Hemisphere (June to August), then travel to Antarctica for summer in the Southern Hemisphere (November to January).

Reindeer, Arctic

In spring, huge herds of reindeer (caribou) head north into the Arctic to feed on lichen and plants. They follow trails that may be hundreds of years old.

Vertical migration

At night, billions of tiny sea creatures swim from the deep to the surface to feed. In the morning, they swim back down. This happens all over the world, even in the Arctic Ocean under thick ice.

Tiny Arctic copepods

Antarctic fur seals, Antarctica

These seals breed on ice-free islands in the summer. Then they migrate out to the ocean in the winter to feed.

Humpback whales, Antarctica

Humpback whales visit Antarctica to feed during summer in the Southern Hemisphere. When winter comes, they head back to warmer waters near the equator to breed.

Do people live here?

The Arctic has long been home to many groups of Indigenous (local) peoples, from several different countries. Today, many non-Indigenous people live there, too. But it's a different story in the Antarctic, since nobody lives here permanently.

Like any other part of the world, the Arctic has many towns and cities. This is Ilulissat, on the west coast of Greenland.

Arctic

Eight countries have northern regions that lie in and around the Arctic Ocean. These countries are Norway, Sweden, Finland, Russia, the United States, Canada, Greenland (part of Denmark), and Iceland.

The Arctic has roads and railways, but they are expensive to build.

green cargo

1138

Antarctic

The Antarctic has no Indigenous population, and it's too cold and remote for people to live there permanently. However, in summer (October to March), around 4,000 scientists and support staff live and work on research bases there.

Skiing is a very popular leisure activity for Antarctic scientists and staff.

In winter, the number of people living in Antarctica falls to around 1,000.

Indigenous traditions

Indigenous peoples have lived in the Arctic for centuries. Among these groups are the Inuit, Sámi, and Chukchi. They developed many different ways to thrive in this unique environment. Today, their lives mix modern living with traditional customs that they pass on to new generations.

Igloo
The Inuit use igloos as temporary shelters on hunting trips.

Sled
Some traditional transport includes kayaks and sleds pulled by dogs.

Food

Arctic peoples have been able to live in this environment by basing their diet around the local animals and plants. In Antarctica, scientists rely on supplies brought in by ships and planes, and on specially grown vegetables.

! **WOW!**

Krill live in **huge swarms,** hundreds of **thousands** strong.

Fish

Fish, such as salmon, Arctic char, and Arctic cod, form a staple part of the diet for people across the Arctic.

Antarctic krill

Krill, a small crustacean, are food for many Antarctic animals. In the last fifty years, people have also started to eat krill.

Sautéed reindeer

In the Arctic, both land and marine mammals are hunted for their meat. They include birds, seals, hares, and reindeer (caribou).

Pomor ukha

The countries around the Arctic Ocean all have their own special dishes. Pomor ukha is a traditional fish soup from Russia.

Snow crab

Snow crabs are prized for the sweet, white meat in their legs and claws. They are caught in the oceans around Alaska.

Cloudberries

Herbs and berries

Different types of berries grow in the Arctic. They include Arctic bramble, bearberries, bilberries, and cloudberries.

Hydroponics

Hydroponics is a way of growing plants in nutrient-rich liquid instead of soil. Research bases in Antarctica have hydroponic chambers where they grow fresh vegetables and herbs. The plants can't survive outside, so they are grown in these chambers to feed the researchers.

Hydroponics chamber

Myth busters

For years, people have been fascinated by the poles, and many ideas have sprung up about what these far-flung places are really like. However, which of these myths are make-believe, and which are based in fact?

There's nothing to do at the poles.

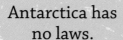

Antarctica has no laws.

Polar bears eat penguins.

It's always winter at the North Pole.

No one lives at the poles.

The Arctic is all ice, snow, and rock.

Wild summer flowers in Arctic Russia

The Arctic has two seasons—a long, cold winter and a short, cool summer.

Far from it! One can try mushing (dog-sledding), skiing, driving a snowmobile, or even kayaking in the ice.

Impossible! Polar bears and penguins live at the opposite ends of the Earth.

There are also grassy meadows, mountains, rivers, lakes, hot springs, and even volcanoes here.

Beerenberg volcano

Antarctic Treaty flags

An Inuit family

No one lives in Antarctica full time, but the Arctic has been home to many different peoples for thousands of years.

The Antarctic Treaty is a set of rules some nations agree to follow in Antarctica.

Polar explorers

Exploring parts of the polar regions can be dangerous because of the extreme conditions and tough terrain. It was particularly hard for the non-native explorers of the 19th century, because they were not used to the environment.

Matthew Henson

Henson was an American explorer. He claimed his 1908–1909 expedition with Robert Peary was the first to reach the North Pole.

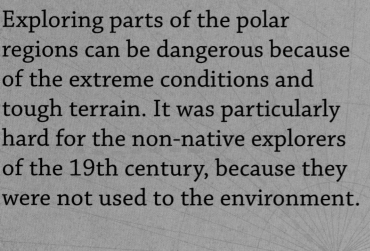

Ernest Shackleton

In 1914, British explorer Ernest Shackleton set off to cross Antarctica by dog sled. His expedition lasted until 1917.

The Inughuit

Many Inughuit people traveled with Robert Peary. They had in-depth knowledge of the area that led the team to successful expeditions.

Who was first?

Foreign explorers have visited the Arctic since the Vikings in the Middle Ages. But the first to come here were Paleo-Eskimo peoples, who journeyed from Eurasia around 4,500 years ago.

Artifacts made by the Thule, who came after the Paleo-Eskimo peoples

 WOW!

Until **the 700s, no one** had ever **seen Antarctica.**

Felicity Aston

British scientist and explorer, Felicity Aston became the first person to ski alone across the Antarctic continent.

Roald Amundsen

One of the greatest polar explorers of all time, Amundsen of Norway led the first team to reach the South Pole on December 14, 1911.

Research stations

The poles are unique places, and scientists come from all over the world to study them. Together with support staff, they live on research stations, equipped with science laboratories, living quarters, gyms, and even greenhouses.

USA's Amundsen-Scott South Pole Station

Bedroom
Everyone living on the base has their own small bedroom, or berth. They share bathrooms, and are only allowed to have two-minute showers.

! WOW!

The building can be **raised up** on its **legs** to keep it clear of the **snow.**

Kitchen
In the kitchen, the chefs prepare four meals a day. These are eaten in the gallery. Everyone takes turns to clean up since there is no dishwasher.

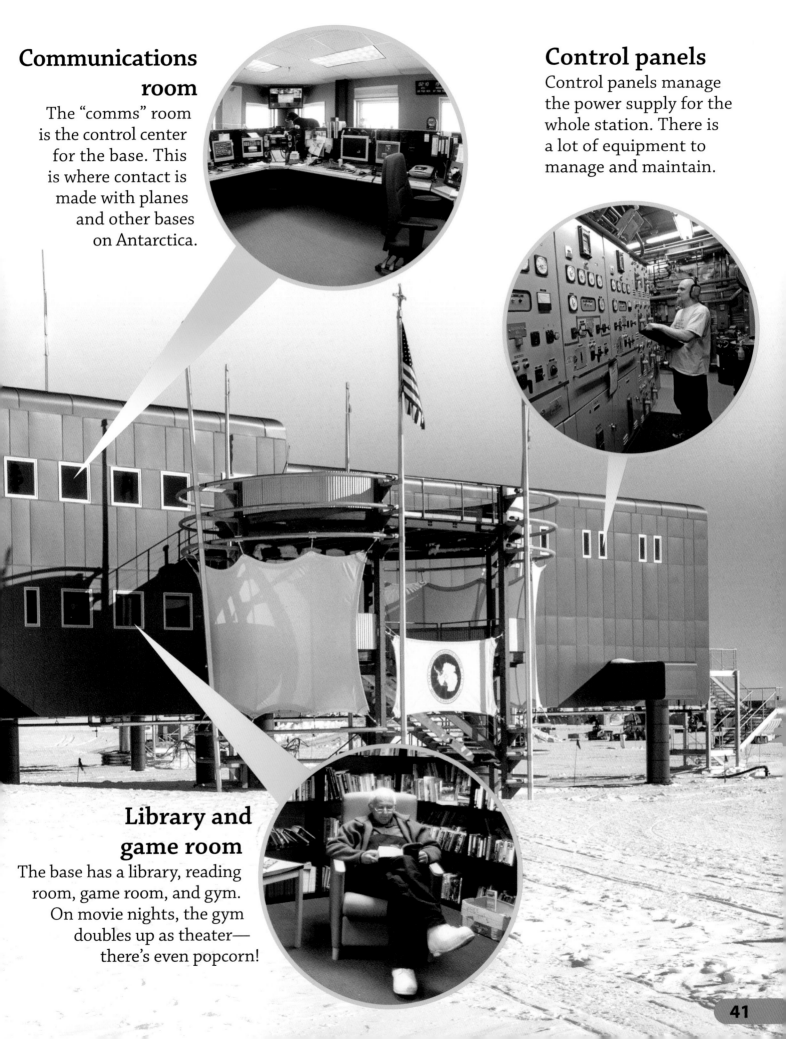

Communications room

The "comms" room is the control center for the base. This is where contact is made with planes and other bases on Antarctica.

Control panels

Control panels manage the power supply for the whole station. There is a lot of equipment to manage and maintain.

Library and game room

The base has a library, reading room, game room, and gym. On movie nights, the gym doubles up as theater— there's even popcorn!

Unusual places

The Arctic and Antarctic are full of surprises. From blood-red waterfalls flowing off glaciers, to a beach of washed-up iceberg shards that sparkle like diamonds, here are just a few of the amazing places to see in the poles.

Lofoten archipelago

Lofoten Islands, Norway

Want to catch a glimpse of the awesome aurora? The Lofoten Islands has some great views of this incredible display.

Diamond-like ice on the sand

Diamond Beach, Iceland

If you're in Iceland, don't miss a chance to visit Diamond Beach. Chunks of icebergs wash up on this strip of black sand, making it shine and sparkle.

The crater of Deception Island

Deception Island, Antarctica

A horseshoe-shaped island in Antarctica, Deception Island is an active volcano. Long ago, its crater collapsed and the ocean flooded in.

Mt. Erebus, Antarctica

Mt. Erebus is an active volcano in icy Antarctica. A lava lake bubbles away in its crater, and steam spouts from vents (cracks) on its sides.

Mt. Erebus on Ross Island

Blood Falls, Antarctica

This waterfall flowing from Taylor Glacier is as high as a five-story building. Its blood-red color comes from a chemical called iron oxide.

Blood Falls

Disko Bay, Greenland

On the west coast of Greenland, Disko Bay is littered with gleaming icebergs. In summer, it's also a brilliant place for watching whales.

Iceberg in Disko Bay

Pole marker

In Antarctica, scientists put up a marker to show the location of the geographical South Pole. They need to change its place every year because the ice underneath keeps shifting.

South Pole marker

Polar escapade

A harp seal pup is born on the Arctic ice. For around 12 weeks, it drinks its mother's milk and grows bigger. Then it is left to look after itself. It faces many threats if it is going to survive.

15 Hooray! You've learned to swim and stay underwater. **Move forward 4 spaces.** Harp seals are excellent swimmers and spend most of their time in water. They can stay underwater for around 15 minutes at a time.

14

START

Catch your first prey

You're a harp seal pup fending for itself. Can you learn to swim in the sea, find your own food, and look out for danger?

1 You're alone. You stay in one place, and live off fat stored under your skin. **Miss a turn.** Seal pups can lose up to half their body weight during the weeks after being weaned.

13 Oh no! You're resting on a chunk of sea ice, and it's melting. **Move back 1 space.** Young pups don't just rest on sea ice. They also feed on small fish around the edges.

6
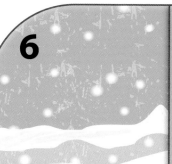

5 A sudden blizzard makes the conditions harsher. **Miss a turn.** Bad weather makes life difficult for the seal pups, who are weak and out in the open.

2

7 You shed your first white fur coat. You're preparing for the sea. **Move forward 1 space.** Seal pups shed their white fur several times before growing their gray adult coat.

4
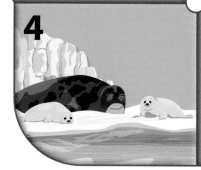

3 You find a huddle of seal pups. You join them to keep warm. **Move forward 3 spaces.** Mother seals leave their pups on the pack ice, until they are ready to hunt for themselves.

12

8

9 Help! A polar bear almost catches you! **Move back 1 space.** Polar bears are the greatest threat to seal pups.

10

11 You've made it to the sea! You're ready to learn to swim. **Move forward 1 space.** At this stage, the pup is called a "beater." It practices beating its tail and flippers in the water.

16

17 A cruise ship passes too close by and almost hits you. **Miss a turn.** The Arctic Ocean has many busy sea routes, and passing ships sometimes injure seals.

18

19

23

22 There's an oil spill in front of you. Take a longer route to the next ice floe. **Go back 1 space.** Oil spills are toxic to seals and their food. They also clog up a seal's skin and coat.

21

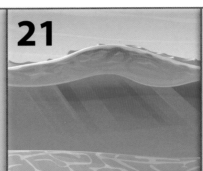

20 You're hungry but you can't find any fish. Where have they all gone? **Move back 1 space.** Overfishing affects the food chain, and leaves seals short of food.

24 At last, you spot a shoal of fish ahead. **Move forward 1 space.** Harp seals mostly eat fish, such as Arctic cod and capelins, and some crustaceans.

25

26 Watch out. A fishing trawler has its net out. You are almost caught. **Miss a turn.** Seals can get tangled up in fishing nets and lines used by fishing fleets.

27

31

30 An orca comes between you and a school of fish. Swim away! **Move back 1 space.** Orcas and Greenland sharks often prey on seals when they are out hunting in deep water.

29

28 All that practice is paying off. You've just made your first deep dive. **Move forward 1 space.** Harp seals are excellent divers, reaching up to 1,300 ft (400 m) deep when hunting.

32 Wow! You've made your first catch. **Move to the FINISH.** Harp seals often hunt for fish in herds.

33

Congratulations! You've faced some deadly dangers, and managed to survive by yourself. Now that you've managed to swim, dive, and hunt, your teeth can start to grow!

FINISH

Natural resources

Many valuable natural resources lie buried beneath the poles. In Antarctica, mining and drilling for oil are banned, but things are very different in the Arctic. The mines, oil pipelines, and refineries here have put the fragile habitat at risk.

Metals

The Arctic is rich in metals, such as copper, nickel, and gold. It can be expensive to mine in this cold climate, but companies can make a lot of money here.

Gold is mined across the Arctic.

Diamonds

Diamonds formed deep inside the Earth, and were carried to the surface by ancient volcanic eruptions. There are large diamond mines in Arctic Russia and Canada.

Most drilling takes place on land.

A natural gas processing plant in Russia

Oil and natural gas

Around a quarter of all the world's oil and natural gas might lie under the Arctic. Drilling can take place on land and at sea.

The Diavik Diamond Mine in northwest Canada

Fresh water

The ice sheet that covers Antarctica contains more than half of the world's total fresh water supply. Another tenth of the world's fresh water is held in the ice that covers Greenland.

Icebergs in Antarctica

Coal

There are vast supplies of coal at both polar regions, and coal has been mined in Arctic Russia and Norway for more than one hundred years.

Most Norwegian mines are now closing.

Norwegian fishermen in the early 20th century

Marine life

Fish, squid, and krill have always been some of the poles' most important natural resources. Millions of tons of marine animals are caught each year.

Poles in peril

The poles are vitally important. Not only are they home to extraordinary animals and millions of people, but they also help to keep our planet's climate in balance. However, human activities are putting both regions under serious threat.

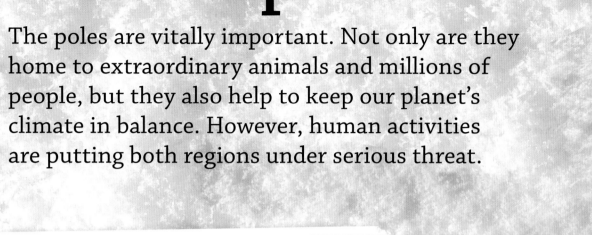

Climate change
Human-made climate change is making the Earth warmer. At the poles, this warming is melting the ice, leading to a rise in sea levels.

Habitat loss
If the ice continues to melt, animals will lose their habitats. Polar bears also hunt for seals on the ice, so less ice means fewer chances to find food.

Overfishing

Fishing can be done in a way that's safe for the environment. But overfishing reduces the population of certain fish, and puts the food chain at risk.

Pollution

Trash dumped in the ocean gets washed up on beaches. Plastic can end up frozen in the ice. Oil can spill from ships and pollute the water.

Industrial activities

Mining and drilling damage fragile polar habitats. Drilling for oil on the seafloor also creates noise, which can be deadly for some sea animals.

Invasive species

Sometimes, plants and animals are brought to the poles from outside. Some, such as red king crabs, can spread very quickly, putting local species at risk.

Endangered animals

Animals at both ends of the Earth face an uncertain future. In the past, large-scale hunting for meat, oil, and furs brought many species to the brink of extinction. Today, climate change is having a devastating effect on the ice, destroying these already fragile habitats.

Polar bear

Polar bears rely on sea ice for hunting, traveling, mating, and making dens. Climate change is causing the ice to melt, putting these animals in great danger.

Beluga whale

One threat facing belugas is noise from shipping, underwater drilling, and construction. This interferes with their use of sound to navigate, find food, and avoid predators underwater.

Walrus

Walruses use sea ice as safe spots to rest and to leave their young while they feed. As the ice melts, they are forced ashore, and face danger from people and predators.

Krill

Krill are an important part of the Antarctic's marine ecosystem. The population is in decline, and this affects many other species, such as crabeater seals, who feed on krill.

Reindeer

Reindeer (caribou) travel long distances to find food, but climate change is affecting their traditional routes. Once-frozen rivers are now melting, and calves can drown as they try to cross.

Albatross

Each year, thousands of seabirds, including some albatross species, are killed by longline fishing in the Southern Ocean. The birds swallow the baited hooks, get caught fast, and drown.

Whale

In the past 100 years, Antarctic blue whales were almost wiped out by commercial whaling. In 1926, there were around 125,000 of these giant whales. By 2018, only about 3,000 were left.

Meet the expert

To learn more about the Arctic, we put some questions to Dr. Mark Serreze. He is the director of the National Snow and Ice Data Center at the University of Colorado Boulder.

Q: What first made you interested in the Arctic?

A: I grew up in Maine where we have real winters, with a lot of snow and ice. I loved sledding, skating, and making snow forts.

Dr. Serreze in the Arctic

Q: What does the National Snow and Ice Data Center (NSIDC) do?

A: We advance the understanding of Earth's frozen regions—known as its cryosphere—and the changes taking place there. This helps with decision-making in service to humanity and Earth. We take great pride in what we do.

Q: What do you love most about your job?

A: I love teaching students about the Arctic, doing research, running NSIDC, and going to the Arctic. There's always something different going on, so it never gets boring.

Q: What has been your favorite experience in the Arctic?

A: It was probably my first visit. I was on top of a little ice cap on a rare clear day and could see probably 50 miles (80 km) in every direction. It was magical.

Q: What do you wish more people knew about the Arctic?

A: The Arctic acts like the planet's refrigerator. Like the Antarctic, the Arctic helps to keep us cool. It also plays a key role in regulating weather.

Q: What can we do to help protect the Arctic?

A: While things like turning out the lights seem very small, they can help us to think differently about how we use energy. We waste so much. Changing the mindset will help us win the battle against climate change.

Meet the expert

To learn more about the Antarctic, we put some questions to Dr. Virginia Morandini. She researches Antarctic wildlife with Oregon State University, with a grant from the U.S. National Science Foundation.

Q: What first made you interested in the Antarctic?

A: I have a strong sense of adventure. I always wanted to be a scientist to help to understand our planet, and I was fascinated by polar exploration and penguins.

Q: What kind of research do you do?

A: Our research focuses on understanding penguin populations and climate change in one of the most remote places on Earth.

Dr. Morandini with Adélie penguins

Q: What do you love most about your job?

A: I love being part of a small crew of scientists isolated for months in Antarctica, working with the biggest Adélie penguin colony on the planet.

Q: What is it like in the Antarctic?

A: Antarctica is the coldest and the windiest continent on the planet, with oceans full of life.

Q: What is a typical day like when you're working in the Antarctic?

A: I wake up in my tent, surrounded by snow. I have breakfast with the crew, and then I spend the day working in the penguin colony.

Q: What has been your favorite experience in the Antarctic?

A: I learned to live in extreme conditions, with no showers, only frozen food, water from melting snow, and sleeping in tents—and I loved it!

Q: What do you wish more people knew about the Antarctic?

A: Antarctica holds most of the world's fresh water and unique wildlife, but commercial fishing and climate change increasingly impact its fragile environments.

Shrinking ice

Climate change is causing the ice at the poles to melt at an alarming rate. Take the Jakobshavn Glacier (shown here), for example. This mighty glacier flows from the Greenland ice sheet into the sea, and it is shrinking fast.

Ice calving
Billions of tons of ice break off the glacier each year as icebergs, but the rate is speeding up. Some of these icebergs are as tall as a 300-story building.

! WOW!

The **iceberg** that sank the *Titanic* came from the **Jakobshavn Glacier!**

Rising sea levels
If the Greenland ice sheet melts completely, it will raise sea levels across the world by around 20 ft (6 m).

Ice loss
In 2010, satellite images showed that the glacier lost enough ice to cover a thousand football fields, in just one day.

Ice rescue

Scientists are working hard to find ways to save the polar ice. One idea is to use robots to build underwater walls to stop warm ocean water from washing against the edges of glaciers.

Underwater robot

Protecting the poles

The Arctic and Antarctic are two of our planet's last great wildernesses, and they play crucial roles in regulating the Earth's temperature. It is vital to protect these fragile habitats and their extraordinary wildlife.

Reducing pollution

Strict laws are in place to reduce pollution at the poles. In Antarctica, non-organic waste from the bases cannot be burned or dumped in the sea. It must be recycled or shipped home.

Picking up litter

Combating climate change

Using green energy, such as wind energy, cuts down on the use of fossil fuels. This latter type of energy that comes from oil and gas adds to global warming.

Wind turbines in Alaska

Caring for critical areas

Many polar animals are losing their homes because their habitats are threatened by climate change. Caring for these places will help save wildlife, such as seals and penguins.

Fur seals and king penguins in Antarctica

Banning mining or drilling

The poles are rich in valuable natural resources, such as coal, but mining or drilling would do lasting damage. Mining in Antarctica is already banned until 2048.

Environmental protestors

Education

From studying in the classroom to doing research on location, learning about the poles is an important step in figuring out how we can protect them.

Doing research

Helping out

Even if you live far from the poles, you can make decisions that help to protect the environment around the world. Try to recycle, and find green ways to get to school, such as walking and cycling.

Everyone can help

Polar facts and figures

The poles are unique environments on the planet, so naturally they're full of surprises! Here are some of the most incredible facts about Earth's amazing polar regions.

Despite its frigid appearance, Antarctica is a **hotbed**. A recent study found **138 volcanoes** in West Antarctica alone!

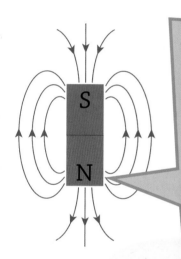

Earth's **magnetic poles** occasionally switch positions. This happens around every **200,000 years**, although the last switch was over 600,000 years ago.

Antarctica's **Victoria Valley** has **sand dunes**!

-144°F

(−97.8°C) is the lowest temperature ever recorded at the highest point in Antarctica.

90

million years ago, Antarctica had sub-tropical forests.

Arctic

comes from the Greek word for bear—*arktos*. It is likely named after the bear-shaped star formations, **the Ursa Major** and **the Ursa Minor**.

The North Pole gets up to **24 hours** of **sunlight** during the **summer**.

Greenland is known as the "Iceberg capital of the World." Every year around **40,000** icebergs break off from Greenland glaciers.

The surface of **Esieh Lake in the Arctic** is always bubbling as it releases around **2 tons (1.8 tonnes) of methane** gas daily—the same as the emissions of **6,000 cows**!

200 ft

61 m) is the height by which sea levels would rise if the Antarctic ice sheet melts. That's nearly as high as a 20-story building!

250

to 400 years is the average lifespan of a Greenland shark. It is the longest-living vertebrate.

Glossary

Here are the meanings of some words that are useful for you to know when learning about the polar regions.

adapt How a living thing changes over time to help it survive in its environment

algae Simple plants found in or near water

antifreeze Special substance in the bodies of some polar fish that stops their blood from freezing

atmosphere Layer of gases around the Earth that protect the planet from the burning rays of the sun

aurora Naturally occurring light displays that happen at the North and South Poles

bacteria Tiny living things that can be found everywhere on Earth, such as inside food, soil, or the human body

blubber Thick layer of fat in some animals that helps to protect them from the cold

calving When an iceberg breaks off the end of an ice sheet or glacier

camouflage Patterns or colors on an animal's skin that help it blend in with the environment

carrion Decaying bodies of dead animals

chemical Substance made by a reaction between particles, such as atoms

climate Weather patterns for a specific area

climate change Process of Earth's climate changing over time

colony Group of animals who live together

crustacean Animal without a backbone that has jointed legs, and often has a hard shell or an exoskeleton

echolocation System used by some animals to find food and navigate, by making sounds that hit an object and measuring how long it takes for an echo to return

ecosystem A community of living things and their environment

endangered Any species of animal or plant that is in danger of dying out

evolve The way living things change and adapt over time to help them survive

forage When animals search for food

fungus A type of living thing, such as a mushroom, that breaks down dead plants and animals to obtain food

glacier Large mass of ice that moves slowly down a slope

global warming When worldwide temperatures rise

green energy Power that comes from sources—such as sunlight or wind—that do not harm the environment and will not run out

habitat Natural home of an animal or plant

hibernate To be in a sleep-like dormant state through the winter

hydroponics chamber Room where plants are grown without the use of soil

invasive species Animals or plants that are brought into a new environment and harm the local wildlife

larvae The young of certain insects, such as wasps

lava Red-hot, melted rock that flows out of a volcano when it erupts

mammal Warm-blooded animal with a backbone that gives birth to live young

marine Sea animals, and the ocean habitat and environment

migration Regular group movement of animals, often to feed or breed

mollusk Animal with a soft body, and often a hard shell, such as a clam

molt When a bird loses its feathers and grows new ones

natural resources Things such as trees, rocks, water, and coal, that are found naturally in a place and are used by people

overfishing Catching so much of a certain type of fish that the population starts to decrease

Paleo-Eskimo The earliest settlers in the Arctic

particle Extremely small part of a solid, liquid, or gas

permafrost A layer of permanently frozen soil under the ground

phytoplankton Tiny algae that live in the sea

pollen Powder that comes from flowering plants and is used in pollination

pollination When insects, such as bees and butterflies, transfer pollen from one plant to another

predator Animal that hunts other living animals for food

prey Animal that is hunted for food

sedge A type of plant

snowdrift Deep pile of snow, formed by the wind

territory The area that an animal considers its own and that it will defend from other animals

treaty Written agreement between countries

vent Opening in the Earth's crust out of which lava, ash, rock, and gas erupt

zooplankton Tiny animals and animal young that float in the sea

Reindeer (caribou)

Index

A

albatross 5, 20–1, 51
Amundsen, Roald 39
Amundsen-Scott South Pole
    Station 40–1
animals 12–31, 26–27, 49,
    50–1, 57, 59
Antarctic 5, 33
Antarctic Treaty 37
antifreeze chemicals 23, 29
Arctic 4, 32, 59
Arctic Ocean 4, 7, 13, 32
Aston, Felicity 39
Aurora Australis 11
Aurora Borealis 10–11
auroras 10–11

B

beluga whales 19, 50
berries 35
birds, polar 20–1, 27, 29,
    30, 51
Blood Falls (Antarctica) 43
blubber 12, 14, 29
blue whales, Antarctic 51
brash ice 7
bumblebees, Arctic 25

C

calving 8, 54
camouflage 16, 17, 28
chinstrap penguins 14
climate change 48, 50, 54–5,
    56, 57
coal 47, 57
colonies 14, 21
conservation 56–7
copepods 31

D

Deception Island
    (Antarctica) 42
desert 5
Diamond Beach
    (Iceland) 42
diamonds 46–7
Disko Bay (Greenland) 43
drilling 49, 57

E

eiders, king 21
elephant seals, southern
    19
emperor penguins 14–15
endangered species 50–1
environment,
    protecting the 56–7
ermines 16
Esieh Lake (USA) 59
explorers, polar 38–9
eyesight 21, 29

F

feathers 14, 15, 21
feet 12, 17, 29
fish 14, 23, 26, 27, 29, 34,
    35, 47, 49
flora 24–5
food 34–5, 47, 50
food web 26–7
fossil fuels 56
foxes, Arctic 17, 28
fresh water 47
fritillary butterflies,
    Arctic 24
fur 12, 16, 17, 28, 50
fur seals, Antarctic 31

G

gas, natural 46, 49, 56
gas particles 10, 11
glaciers 6, 8, 54–5, 59
global warming 48, 56
green energy 56
Greenland 4, 6, 32, 43, 47,
    54–5, 59
ground squirrels, Arctic 17

H

habitat loss 48, 50, 57
hairgrass, Antarctic 25
hares, Arctic 28
Henson, Matthew 38
herbs 35
Hoff crabs 23
huddles 5, 15, 18, 28
human activity 48–9
humpback whales 26, 31
hunting 12, 13, 16, 21, 27,
    33, 34, 48, 50
hydroponics 35

I

ice caps 6
ice floes 7
ice sheets 4, 6, 8, 47, 54–5
ice shelves 6
icebergs 8–9, 54, 59
icefish, Antarctic 23
igloos 33
Indigenous peoples 32–3,
    37
insects 23, 24–5
Inughuit people 38
Inuit people 33, 37
invasive species 49

J

Jakobshavn Glacier 54–5

K

kayaks 33, 37
krill 14, 26, 27, 34, 47,
    50–1

L

land ice 6–7
leopard seals 14, 19
lichens 5
lion's mane jellyfish 22
litter pickup 56, 57
Lofoten Islands
    (Norway) 4

M

magnetic field, Earth's 10
magnetic poles 58
mammals, land 16–17
mammals, marine 18–19
melting ice 6, 9, 26, 48, 50,
    51, 54–5, 59
metals 46
midges, Antarctic 24
migration 30–1
mining 49, 57
molting 15
Morandini, Virginia 53
Mount Erebus
    (Antarctica) 43
Murmansk (Russia) 32
musk oxen 16–17, 28
myths 36–7

N

narwhals 19
National Snow and
    Ice Data Center 52–3
natural resources 46–7,
    57
North Pole 4, 59

O

oil 46, 49, 56
orcas 14, 27
overfishing 49

P

pack ice 7
Paleo-Eskimo peoples 39
pancake ice 7
pearlwort, Antarctic 25
Peary, Robert 38
Penguin Science 53
penguins 5, 14–15, 20, 22,
    28, 37
permafrost 7
phytoplankton 26
plants 5, 24–5, 26, 35, 49
plastic pollution 49
play-fighting 13
polar bears 12–13, 22, 27,
    28, 37, 48, 50
polar regions 4–5
pollution 49, 56
pomor ukha 35
poppies, Arctic 25
ptarmigan 28
puffins, Atlantic 21

R

recycling 56, 57
reindeer (caribou) 34, 51
research stations 33, 34, 35,
    40–1, 56
robots, underwater 55

S

sand dunes 58
saxifrage, purple 24
scientists 33, 34, 39, 40–1
sea ice 6–7
sea levels, rising 48, 55, 59
sea spiders, Antarctic 23
seabirds 20–1, 27, 30, 51

seals 12, 13, 14, 19, 26, 31, 48
seasons 37
Serreze, Mark 52
Shackleton, Ernest 38
sharks, Greenland 59
skiing 33, 37, 39
skuas, south polar 20
sleds 33, 37
snow crabs 35
snowy owls 21, 28
solar particles 10, 11
South Pole 4, 43
Southern Ocean 5, 23
springtails, Antarctic 22
squid 27, 47
sun 4, 10, 59
survival 28–9

T

temperatures 4, 56, 58
terns, Arctic 27, 30
Titanic 54
trash 49
tusks 18, 19

V

vegetation 5
vents 23
vertical migration 31
Vikings 39
volcanoes 5, 37, 58

W

walruses 18, 26, 50
whales 19, 26, 31, 50, 51
wolverines 16–17
woolly bear caterpillars,
    Arctic 23

Z

zooplankton 27

Acknowledgments

The publisher would like to thank the following people for their assistance in the preparation of this book: Caroline Bingham for proofreading; Helen Peters for compiling the index; Dr. Mark Serreze for his "Meet the expert" interview and photographs; Dr. Virginia Morandini for her "Meet the expert" interview; and Arvind Varsani and Amélie Lescroel for the photographs on page 53.

The publisher would like to thank the following for their kind permission to reproduce their photographs:

(Key: a-above; b-below/bottom; c-center; f-far; l-left; r-right; t-top)

1 Dreamstime.com: Fonciw (b); Yasushitanikado (cb).
2 Dorling Kindersley: Natural History Museum London / Harry Taylor (crb/X3). Dreamstime.com: Noahgolan (crb/Plate). 2–3 Alamy Stock Photo: All Canada Photos / Wayne Lynch (bc); imageBROKER (cb). 3 Dreamstime.com: Mutabor5 (tc); Vladsilver / Vladimir Seliverstov (br); David Pereiras Villagra (crb). 4 Dreamstime.com: Rgbe (cla); Vladsilver / Vladimir Seliverstov (bc). 5 Dreamstime.com: Andrea Basile (cr); Vladimir Seliverstov (clb); Sophia Granchinho (tc); Tarpan (ca); Alexey Sedov (br). Shutterstock.com: Sergej Onyshko (tr). 6 Alamy Stock Photo: Andy Myatt (clb). Dreamstime.com: Steven Prorak (ca). Getty Images: Mario Tama (br). NASA: (r). 7 Alamy Stock Photo: Michel & Gabrielle Therin-Weise (l). Dreamstime.com: Achim Baqué (crb); David Dennis (tl); Tenedos (bl). naturepl.com: Jeff Vanuga (cra). 9 NASA. 10–11 Dreamstime.com: Alexander Shalamov. 10 Dreamstime.com: Simone Renoldi (crb). 11 Alamy Stock Photo: mauritius images GmbH / Arctic-Images (crb). Dreamstime.com: Paul Sparks (clb). 12 Science Photo Library: POWER AND SYRED (bl). 12–13 Getty Images / iStock: Alexey Seafarer. 13 Alamy Stock Photo: Martin Smart (cb). Getty Images / iStock: Marcusd (cr). Shutterstock.com: Elena Birkina (tc). 14 Dreamstime.com: Barbarico (bl). Getty Images: Wolfgang Kaehler (cl). 14–15 Dreamstime.com: Merggy. Shutterstock.com: vladsilver (c). 15 Alamy Stock Photo: All Canada Photos / Glenn Bartley (crb); imageBROKER / Konrad Wothe (tr). 16 Alamy Stock Photo: McPhoto / Rolf Mueller (bl). 16–17 Dreamstime.com: Lanaufoto (bc); Karine Patry (tc). 17 Alamy Stock Photo: Michael Lingberg (tr). Getty Images: DmitryND (br). 18 Alamy Stock Photo: Arterra Picture Library / Arndt Sven-Erik (b). 19 Alamy Stock Photo: McPHOTO / PUM / blickwinkel (cr). Dreamstime.com: Planetfelicity (tr); Vladimir Seliverstov (b). Shutterstock.com: Luna Vandoorne (cl). 20 Dreamstime.com: Mutabor5 (cra). 20–21 Dreamstime.com: Goldilock Project (b). 21 Dreamstime.com: Agami Photo Agency (br); Tomas1111 (cla). Getty Images / iStock: E+ / pchoui (cra). 22 naturepl.com: David Hall (cl). Science Photo Library: BRITISH ANTARCTIC SURVEY (crb). 23 Alamy Stock Photo: Minden Pictures / Norbert Wu (br). Dreamstime.com: Debra Millet (tl). naturepl.com: Jordi Chias (cra). PLoS Biology: (clb). 24 Dreamstime.com: Andrei Stepanov (b). Richard E. Lee Jr.: (cl). Shutterstock.com: Incredible Arctic (cra); Jukka Jantunen (crb); Jukka Jantunen (cb). 25 Alamy Stock Photo: All Canada Photos / Wayne Lynch (tl); Mim Friday (cr); era-images / Colin Harris (br). Dreamstime.com: Viktoria Ivanets (bl). 26 Alamy Stock Photo: LWM / NASA / LANDSAT (cra); WaterFrame mus (clb). Dreamstime.com: Rixie (crb); Vladsilver / Vladimir Seliverstov (bc). 27 Alamy

Stock Photo: imageBROKER (crb). Dreamstime.com: Mandimiles (bl); Slowmotiongli (fcl); Slowmotiongli (cl); Slowmotiongli (clb); Alexey Sedov (br). NTNU/UNIS: GeirJohnsen (tl). 28 Getty Images / iStock: E+ / Justinreznick (cra). Getty Images: Universal Images Group Editorial / Auscape (cl). Shutterstock.com: Holly S Cannon (crb). 29 Alamy Stock Photo: Design Pics Inc / Alaska Stock RF / Doug Lindstrand (cra). Dreamstime.com: Alexei Poselenov (cl). Getty Images / iStock: lightpix (tr); zanskar (bl). Simon Morley: (crb). 30 Dreamstime.com: Vladimir Melnikov (r). Getty Images / iStock: Alphotographic (l). 31 Alamy Stock Photo: Krys Bailey (l); Minden Pictures / Flip Nicklin (tr). Getty Images / iStock: E+ / lindsay_imagery (r). 32 Dreamstime.com: Vadim Nefedov (cl). Getty Images / iStock: BeyondImages (b). 33 Alamy Stock Photo: Ashley Cooper (cla); H. Mark Weidman Photography (cr). Dreamstime.com: 9parusnikov (cb); Hel080808 (crb). 34 Alamy Stock Photo: ian nolan (clb/Char); Sunrise (br). Dorling Kindersley: Natural History Museum London / Harry Taylor (cra/X3). Dreamstime.com: Fedbul (clb); Robyn Mackenzie (clb/Plate); Noahgolan (cra/Plate). Getty Images / iStock: andyKRAKOVSKI (cl). 35 Dreamstime.com: Iulianna Est (cr); Boris Ryzhkov (tc); Evgenii Mitroshin (cra X2); Eyeblink (cl). Courtesy of the National Science Foundation: TSgt Timothy Russer, USAF (br). 37 Alamy Stock Photo: Arterra Picture Library / Keirsebilck Patrick (cr); H. Mark Weidman Photography (br). Dreamstime.com: Anyaberkut (tr); Andrei Stepanov (tl). Getty Images: National Science Foundation / Handout / Rob Jones (clb). Shutterstock.com: FloridaStock (ca). 40–41 Depositphotos Inc: sergeydolya. 40 Courtesy of the National Science Foundation: Calee Allen, NSF (ca); Kristan Hutchison (br). 41 Alamy Stock Photo: Eye Ubiquitous (cra). Courtesy of the National Science Foundation: Keith Morel (tc); Emily Stone (bc). 42 123RF.com: Jan Novak (tr). Dreamstime.com: Nicoelnino (cl). Shutterstock.com: evenfh (crb). 43 Alamy Stock Photo: Zoonar GmbH / LUXart (clb). Dreamstime.com: Darryn Schneider (bc); Martyn Unsworth (tl). Courtesy of the National Science Foundation: Peter Rejcek, NSF (cra). 44 Alamy Stock Photo: Dolores Harvey (bl); Nature Picture Library / Jurgen Freund (crb). Dreamstime.com: Anastasiya Aheyeva (cra, clb); Yukitama (cr); Anthony Hathaway (bc). 45 Alamy Stock Photo: Nature Picture Library / Doug Allan (tl). Dreamstime.com: Artinspiring (cla); Cat Vec (tr); VetraKori (cra); Dima1970 (c); Julia Kutska (cr); Slowmotiongli (clb). Getty Images: Moment Open / Carl Conway (crb). Shutterstock.com: Dolores M. Harvey (bl). 46 123RF.com: picsfive (t). Dreamstime.com: Ijp2726 (cra); Chonticha Wat (c); Ijp2726 (cra/Pink); Robyn Mackenzie / Robynmac (br). Shutterstock.com: FUCKtograff (bl). 47 Alamy Stock Photo: All Canada Photos / Jason Pineau (tl); Zoonar GmbH / Gualtiero Boffi (cr). Dreamstime.com: Guido Amrein (cla); Awcnz62 (bl). 48–49 123RF.com: Koba Samurkasov. 48 Dreamstime.com: Biserko (cl); Paul Van Slooten (bc). 49 123RF.com: picsfive (bl). Alamy Stock Photo: Global Warming Images / Ashley Cooper (cra); imageBROKER / Andrey Nekrasov (clb). Dreamstime.com: Traderphotos (br). NOAA: (tl). 50 Alamy

Stock Photo: Stocktrek Images Inc / Steve Jones (tr). Dreamstime.com: Alexey Sedov (cr). Shutterstock.com: CJ Larsen (bl); wildstanimal (br). 51 Depositphotos Inc: mic1805 (b). Dreamstime.com: Martin Schneiter (cl). Getty Images / iStock: lightpix (cr). 52 Dreamstime.com: Andamanse. 53 Dreamstime.com: Marc-andré Le Tourneux. 54–55 Getty Images: Monica Bertolazzi. 55 Dreamstime.com: Papa1266 (cra). 56 Alamy Stock Photo: Ashley Cooper pics (clb); peace portal photo (crb). Dreamstime.com: Ferli Achirulli Kamaruddin (cb). 57 Alamy Stock Photo: Cheryl Ramalho (tc); US Senate (c); TASS / Yuri Smityuk (crb). Dreamstime.com: David Pereiras Villagra (br). 58 Alamy Stock Photo: Mountain Light / Galen Rowell (cr). 58–59 Dreamstime.com: Ekaterina Mikhailova. 59 Alamy Stock Photo: WorldFoto (cr). Dreamstime.com: Chernetskaya (clb); Magann / Markus Gann (tr); Mourad Mourinou (clb/Cows); Tawatchai Prakobkit (clb); Planetfelicity (br). 60 Alamy Stock Photo: Mim Friday (tl). 61 Getty Images / iStock: lightpix (br). 62 Dreamstime.com: Simone Renoldi (tl). 64 Depositphotos Inc: mic1805 (tl).

Endpaper images: Front: Alamy Stock Photo: Chronicle , Classic Image tl, IanDagnall Computing bc, IanDagnall Computing cb, PA Images tr; Dreamstime.com: Nigel Spiers bl; The Ohio State University Libraries: Byrd Polar and Climate Research Center Archival Program, Admiral Richard E. Byrd Papers cr; Shutterstock.com: ANL br; Back: Dreamstime.com: Ernest Akayeu tl, Artinspiring bl, Vladislav Lukyanov br, Macrovector tl (Woman), clb, Makarovstock crb, Evgenii Naumov cra, Pavlo Syvak cla, Vatrushka67 tr.

Cover images: Front: Alamy Stock Photo: Mim Friday cla, Imagebroker / Arco / TUNS b, WaterFrame_mus crb; Dreamstime.com: Alexander Shalamov ca, Chonticha Wat c, Marcin Wojciechowski cra; Getty Images: Daniel Parent tc; Back: Dreamstime.com: Anyaberkut crb, Iulianna Est cla, Lanaufoto bl; Getty Images: David Tipling / Digital Vision tr; Spine: Dreamstime.com: Marcin Wojciechowski.

All other images © Dorling Kindersley
For further information see: www.dkimages.com